AFGHAN
WAR
2021

AFGHAN
WAR
2021

STEPHEN W. SWEIGART

ISBN 978-1-957582-72-6 (paperback)
ISBN 978-1-957582-73-3 (eBook)

Printed in the United States of America

W E S T P O I N T
PRINT AND MEDIA

On August 15, 2021, the Taliban entered Kabul.
The United States puppet elected President
In Sept. 2014, re-elected 2019.
Ashraf Ghani,
An anthropologist, who taught university in USA.
Fled to the UAE (United Arab Emirates).
The fall of Kandahar, the second largest city
Made it emanant that the Taliban advance
To Kabul, the capital.

Zabiullah Mujahid, spokesperson for Taliban
promises inclusive government,
security for agencies, and
embassies, and women rights
to work and go to school —
within his groups interpretation
of sharia law.

Chaos breaks out at airport,
with many wanting to leave.
The United States begins
airlifting USA citizens
and supporters of invasion of USA Afghan War.

Sharia law based on the Quran,
Sunnah, authentic hadith; qiyas, analogical reasoning.
Ijma, judicial consensus.
Fqih, jurisprudence; rituals and
mu amulet, social relations.
In many cases capital punishment.

Like most religions it based on fictious laws
Another world. A mythology.

Joe Biden, President of the United States of America.
Followed former President Donald Trump's
Timeline for withdrawal of troops. August 31st, 2021.

US commercial airlines to facilitate to move
evacuees from temporary sites
of Afghanistan.

13 USA service members killed
In attack at Kabul airport,
And more than 60 Afghans died
140 wounded.
After State Department warned
Of attacks from extremist groups.

Zabiullah Mujahid said
That "no extension"
Will be accepted of August 31st deadline
For USA to leave,
Taliban eager to formally establish
New government.in Afghanistan.

101,300 people from Kabul.
96, 000 in past 12 days'
On Wednesday, the Taliban
Instructed that no more
Afghans could depart from the country.
The incident at Hamid Karzai
International Airport
Provoked the State Department
To transmit alert "…US citizens should leave immediately."

The military is planning the entire
Withdrawal from Kabul airport
By August 31st
All weapons, helicopters, vehicles, and
5,000 US troops.
The local state official,
The anti-Taliban leader
Ahmad Masoud
Ask Russia to prevent escalation
Of violence in the Panjshir Valley.
"If government is inclusive then we can
Look at the future with hope."

George W. Bush in September 2001,
A mutual resolution
To use force for those deemed accountable
For the attack on USA on September 11, 2001.
The legal rationale for his decision
To take far-reaching actions
To combat terrorism.
Sets up a detention camp in Guantanamo Bay, Cuba.

After the loss at Mazar-e-Sharif
On Nov. 9 forces loyal
To Abdala Rashid Dostum
An ethnic Uzbek military leader.
The security council
Passes 'Resolution 1378,'
Calling for 'central rule'
For United Nations

In 2021 August 27,
Phil Murphy Governor of New Jersey
Orders a task force to receive
And welcome those airlifted
From Kabul airport.
Arriving in Philadelphia International Airport,
To be processed and housed
At Military Bases In New Jersey.

This is typical of liberals and capitalist conservatives.
To let the working class and
And small businesses pay for those imported,
Taking on good paying jobs
As future voters.
The Taliban has stated they need
People in Afghanistan.
This is a situation
Is like the Berlin Wall,
That tried to prevent citizens
To leave Socialist counties
From being bribed in name of freedom.

An Afghan security guard was killed Monday
In a shootout
Outside Kabul airport.
In a scene as described as frenetic.
As thousands of people scramble for a way out of country.
20 more US military planes sent.

Taliban spokesperson Suhail Shaheed spoke:
That additional time would not be awarded,
To continue evacuations after Aug. 31st.

After tracking Bin Laden
To a cave complex in Tora Bora
Southeast of Kabul
Militia involved in a fierce
Two-week battle with al-Qaeda Dec 3rd to 17th.
Bin Laden escaped to Pakistan on horseback
It is thought.

August 27, 2010

The US military drone strike
Killed two "two
"High profile"
Islamic State militants.

"The Americans should have informed us
Before conducting their air strikes.
It is clearly an attack on Afghan territory."
A Taliban spokesperson said.
The Taliban have arrested suspects
Involved in airport blast.

According to the Watson Institute 177,000
Afghan and Pakistani civilians
Were killed since 2001.
George W. Bush, Barack Obama,
And Mitchell McConnell Jr.
Justifies it.

On December 5, 2001, the Interim government.

The United Nations invited Afghan factions
Most prominently the Northern Alliance,
And the group led by the former King,
The Taliban was not included.
The Bonn, Germany Agreement was signed
By factions, and
The United Nations endorsed by
Resolution 1383.
On December 9, the Taliban surrendering
And its leader Kahayan Mullah Omar, flees.
Al-Qaeda leaders continue
To hide out in the mountains.
Operation Anaconda, the first major
Ground assault against
Eight hundred al-Qaeda and Taliban fighters
In the Shah-I-kot Valley
2,000 US and a 1,000 Afghan troops
Battle the militants.

The Pentagon planners began shifting
Military and intelligence recourses
The chief threat "was on terror"

Bernie Sanders the Senator from Vermont
First entered the House of Representative
In 1991, and the Senate in 2007.
People complain about Putin, but he has been
In power for 30 years. I am sure that
Many of his opponents feel
he is much the same.

Since has begun his hot air speeches.
The situation of the lower middle class
Has gotten worst.

April 17, 2002, reconstructing Afghanistan.
George W. Bush in a speech
At the Virginia Military Institute
"By helping to build an Afghanistan
That is free from evil and
Is a better place in which to live?
We are working in the best
Tradition of George Marshall."
The US Congress approves
Over $38 billion in humanitarian and
Reconstruction assistance 2001 to 2009.

If the USA really wanted to help
The Afghan people it would not
Impose its will, religious and economic
Beliefs on the Afghans. That is why
The Taliban has power.

Phil Murphy, the Governor of New Jersey
Tweets that everyone should
Have the right free attendance
To Community College.
This is subsidized paid now through
Property Tax into County paid in
Local Townships or Boroughs.
Now who will pay for this?
The retired, and citizens, property owners (tenants)
Businesses.

America's longest War is finished.
The final soldiers entered
The last military transports.
To depart country.
Before August 31st deadline.

Spokesman Zabiullah Mujahid
Spoke to reporters at the airport.
"This victory belongs to all."
"We liberated our country
From aggressive power."
The United States airlifted
More than 123,000 people
Including 6,000 American citizens.

"Human rights will be the center
Of our foreign policy, but
The way to do that is not through
Endless military employments
But through diplomacy, economic tools
And rallying the rest of the world
for support." Biden said.

'Pot head' Cory Booker, the senator
From New Jersey.
Talks and tweets about legalizing marijuana
In the Federal government.
But does not about judicial reform
In the counties of New Jersey.
Courts are back up, with lack of judges,
Privilege for lawyers, and bureaucracy.
The jails are condition ghastly,
And food is horrible.

"The last five aircraft have left "it's over"
Said Hamad Shehsad, Taliban fighter
"I cannot express my happiness in words…
Our 20 years of sacrifice worked"

Now the Taliban controlled all of Afghanistan
Except for the mountain valley
Of Panjshir province
Here a few thousand fighters' resist.
The Taliban promises a peaceful resolution.

A series of attacks by the Islamic State
extremist group's barrage
of rockets at airport Monday.
Shows the security challenge
Taliban face.
More civilians were killed
In US-drone attacks.
September 3rd.
Taliban forces take full control,
Resistance in Panjshir valley halted.
Celebrating gunfire heard in Kabul, the capital.

UAE plane first plane to arrive after withdrawal,
along with Aid.

Neighbor calls police after his son,
Sees someone approach my car 12:30 am.
Camera I installed only catches flashlight,
I increase length of detection sensor.

I have lived in same home
In Cherry Hill, NJ, since 1985.
I enjoy living near Cherry Hill Mall.
Close to work and the shopping district.
I was born at former West Jersey Hospital
In Camden.
In the apartments after World War II,
Off Kings Hwy. before Haddonfield.

I have lived a dorm at Xavier University
In 1967-1968.
On Appletree St. in Philadelphia,
Renting a room.
Then purchased a home in Collingswood, NJ.
1975-1979.
Lived in an apartment in Maple Shade, NJ
1979-1980.
Returned to my parents in Cherry Hill, NJ
1980-1985.

China has become the principal partner,
and a gateway to global markets.
They are ready to invest in reconstruction.
Taliban spokesperson has declared.

On Sunday aid from planes
from Qatar and Bahrain
arrived in Kabul
conveying more than fifty tons
of medical aid and food products.

A small group of women
Have presented protest in
Three separate locations.
As they approached the Taliban guards
Responded to their approach
"We will pass the message on to the elders"
As they approached the Presidential palace,
They were prevented.

Until the 19th century women in the West
Were suppressed by religions
And governments.
Women fought for their rights.
Today women are still suppressed
The way to this is I am not sure
Like the demonstrations
On the White House in USA.

May 2003
Secretary of Defense Donald Rumsfeld
Declares an end to "major combat."
President George W, Bush
"Mission accomplished"
Affirmation end of fighting in Iraq.
President Hamid Karzai
"Have concluded that we are at a point
Where we are clearly have moved
From major combat activity
To a period of stability and
Stabilization and reconstruction
And activities.
8,000 US troops occupy.

August 8, 2003
The North Atlantic Treaty Organization (NATO)
In Afghanistan assumes command
Of International security presence across the country.
In 2006, the ISAF accepts command
Of military forces
In Eastern Afghanistan and
Becomes more concerned
In war in Southern portion.

The Taliban are allowing women
To enter universities.
Abaya robes an attend and niqab,
If they attend, and there is segregation.
Most Taliban women are happy
To go back wearing hijab.
This is progress and influence
For more rights in future.
Hijab is covering the head,
Ears and neck, the face is visible.
As wore by most women in Muslim world.

It is reported that the Pentagon
Has spent $1 billion
On the Family Advocacy Program
For domestic abuse victims
Since 2015 but survivors
Say they cannot get help.
100,000 incidents since 2015
In military.
No one went to trial.
Abused women have difficulties
Search for employment.
Not being able to see their children
Having them taken from you
Having to seek employment.

It must be remembered that profits
Are made off 'masks'
By mostly 'Do-gooders' and Capitalist.

Taliban accuses US of violating Doha Agreement.
For keeping the new interior minister
Sirajuddin Haqqani on US terror list.
Including Prime Minister
Mullah Mohamad Hassid Akhund
Are black-listed internationally.

George W. Bush and Hamid Karzai
Issues a joint affirmation
To give access to Afghan military
To resources to prosecute
"Against violent extremist."
"To strengthen US Afghanistan
Ties and help ensure
Afghanistan develops the capacity
To undertake this responsibility
To rebuild the country's
Economy and political democracy."

Qatar bestows, technical assistance,
Along with Turkey,
To revive the airport
After damaged by US troops.
The Taliban government faces
Economic challenges.
Qatari foreign minister met
With Prime Minister Hasan Akhund.
The Taliban had a political office
the Qatar flew first international
Flights, international flights
Out of Kabul airport.
Televisions now remain,
As well as news channels
With female broadcasters.

In July 2006 surge in fighting
Activated in south
Suicide strikes quadrupled
Remote detonation bombings doubled.
Despite election.
These individuals were barred
From government.
And could not take part in elections.

In my yard raccoons, skunks, squirrels,
rabbits, birds, and other creatures.

November 2006 NATO Secretary-General
Jaap de Hoop Schaeffer
Issues target for 2008
National Afghan Army to secure
Central security.
US Secretary of Defense Robert Gates
Criticizes NATO countries, late 2007...

May 2007 Taliban military commander
Mullah Dad Ullah is killed by
Afghan, NATO, and US armed forces
In Helmand Province.

August 27, 2008
Afghan and UN investigations
Found a rising number of civilians killed
General Stanley A McChrystal
Commands overhaul of US air strikes
Methods.

February 2017, 2009
US President Barack Obama
Intends to send seventeen thousand
More troupes, to war zone.

Obama announces Afghanistan
Is more important than Iraq,
And withdraws troops.

As of January 2009
The Pentagon has
Thirty-seven thousand troops
Divided by NATO and US.

"The Taliban acting foreign minister
Amir Khan Mutta qi,
Thanks world pledging hundreds
For pledging hundreds of millions
Dollars in emergency aid to Afghanistan
And urges the United States
To show "heart"
To the impoverished country"
AFP (Agency France Presse)

US drone assaults in Afghanistan
August 29 killed
as many as ten civilians and
not a single ISIS-K member.
General Frank McKenzie,
The commander
Of US Central Command,
Called it "a tragic mistake"

Actions like this only make Afghan and
Those that already oppose us,
Hate us more.

New York Governor who replaced
Governor Cuomo
Kathy Hochu on Friday
Ordered the speedy release
Of inmates at Rikers Island.
"Our fellow New Yorkers users on parole
That is a point of shame for us
And it needs to be fixed.
It is going to be fixed today."

'Justice for J6' rally.
610 parties federally charged
For involvement on January 6, protest
At US Capitol, sixty are held behind bars.
Many in far right warned supporters
To avoid demonstrations.
The government has always filmed
And black listed.
As they did on January 6.
The FBI, Homeland Security,
And Congress of US.

The drinking of enormous amounts of liquid
Is essential to good health.
Eight hours of sleep is not necessary
And even harmful, each day.
Washing ones faces several times
Prevents sickness.

"For propagation of virtue and prevention of vice"
As the Taliban put together a new ministry.
- Leading out World Bank staff members.

March 27, 2009, President Obama
Reveals new strategy
For war effort "to disrupt, dismantle, and
Defeat al Qaeda and its haven
In Pakistan or Afghanistan"
Urges increase in aid to Pakistan
And four thousand more troops.
President Hamid Karzai welcomes policy.
May 11, 2009. Highest commander in Afghanistan
Is now General Stanley A. McChrystal
"A fresh thinking" and "fresh eyes" and
An approach "aggressive and innovative"
Is essential to Afghan War
With more attention on 'counterinsurgency.'

More than 20 years ago a psychiatrist
Began stop taking Health Insurance
Then he began telling his patients that
That they needed to be evaluated
For sleep disorder: Sleep Apnea.
I saw this a scheme to make profits
By Capitalist.

President Biden delivered a speech
the United Nations
General Assembly on pandemic.
"Our shared grief is a poignant reminder
That our collective future
Will hinge on our ability
To respond to a common humanity."

Melbourne *Earthquake*, Australia
The agreement for nuclear submarines
Was signed a few days before.

Hurricane 'IDA' was one of worst disasters
In New Jersey history
A storm like *'Sandy.'*

In Spring 2015 while in a great visit to Athens
For 10 days, I visited the Forum a few times.
I took pictures of reconstruction in an area.
Signs were posted photos not allowed.
In airport on the return to Rome, Italy.
My cell phone disappeared
Or was lost. I merely went to police
To report this for possible
That it was missing.

It is obvious that after my present research
On Afghanistan War.
That Vice President Biden was a 'servant'
To President Baraka Obama
Therefore, I was Lukewarm to his candidacy.
I was never happy that little
Done for New Jersey, Delaware being
Neighboring state.

In April 2009 US officials
Call on NATO members
To develop Afghan civil society
Reconstruction.
5,000 more troops
To train Afghan army
For Presidential election.

November 2009 Presidential Elections
On August 20, President Hamid Karzai
Was marred with fraud.
A runoff election was necessary
No candidate had over 50%.
Then one candidate

December 1, 2009
Obama in a
National televised speech
Pledges 30,000 more troops
A top of 68,000 already there.
"Will increase our ability to train
A competent Afghan security force."
Says Nation interest are related to success
Of Afghan War.

June 23, 2010, General Stanley McChrystal
Let go of his post
As commander of US forces in Afghanistan.
President Obama designates
General David Petraeus.
"This is a change in personnel.
Not a change in policy."

An advertisement appeared on
New Jersey television
Stating that the New Jersey Drug (medicine) industry
Was innovative and if progressives
Plan to socialize would obstruct
The present industry.
The scientists are those who create
Not Capitalist Bosses.
Who are responsible for deaths?
From giving 'kick backs' (monetary reimbursement) to doctors
For prescribing medicine
And lobbyist In Congress.
Preventing lower prices,
Mass deaths.

November 2010 In Lisbon NATO members
Sign affirmation
To hand over obligations
To Afghan forces in 2014.

May 1, 2011, Osama bin Laden killed
In Pakistan by US forces
The US claimed he is accountable
For 911 attacks he denied it.
President Hamid Karzai
States   "For years we have said that
The fight against terrorism
Is not in Afghanistan villages and houses."

June 22, 2011, President Obama
outlines plan to withdraw 30,000 troops
by summer of 2012
Polls show that American people
Do not back War.
Preliminary peace talks begin with Taliban leadership.

When Jimmy Carter ran for re-election
Ted Kennedy ran against him.
I made radio statements against Kennedy
Even though I had difference with Carter.
I believe Ted Kennedy had me arrested
I defended myself and did not resist.
I was picked up outside my apartment.
Ted Kennedy lost Jimmy Carter to Reagan.

I have always received mail
From Carter Center, never from Kennedy.
Now Kennedy Hospital was renamed
In the past few years.
In Cherry Hill, to Jefferson.

My Social Security was taken from me
While I could not place bail
In 2015-16, no phone numbers
Since my cell and computer confiscated,
Yet I pay property tax for the county jail.

After not receiving my inheritance
Rent money. I broke a glass window
And spray painted door.
I was arrested for criminal charges
Represented myself and won.
Lowered to civil matter.
Yet this was prevented from occurring.

Phil Murphy, the Governor of New Jersey
Is a 'punk' of the Capitalist
They pay him good to conduct their agenda.
His Mansion in Princeton
And villa In Europe.

October 7, 2011, the tenth year of Afghanistan War
President Obama plans withdrawal
Of all combat troops.
Pakistan according to US
Undermines efforts
Providing a haven
Opponents.
The US public support is dwindling
And economic downturn
And 9.1 unemployment rate
$1.3 trillion annual budget.

President Karzai suspended discussions
after Budnamed Rabbani
is government chief negotiator.

December 5, 2011, In Bonn, Germany
Conference to discuss political future'
Of Afghanistan.

Jeffery Nash was elected in 1991
as freeholder [commissioner]
of Camden County.
He is responsible for Courts and Jails.
Does he give damn about Property tax?
being high or why do we need a county police.
We have local police.
The jails have horrible food
Mostly potatoes.
No teeth hygiene.
In hospitals phone numbers
Are available.
My cell phone was confiscated by US Customs'
I could not call anyone.
Twenty-three half hours in cell only half hour
Watching Television.
Still no court date after three months.
No paper or pen to write
Or access to addresses.
Collect calls only.
Courts without a lawyer you sit on bench
While lawyers have privileged seats.
Judges favor Capitalist lawyers.

March 2012 Taliban rescind talks.
Accidental burning of Qurans
By US troops
Accusation of murdering
sixteen Afghan villagers.
Hamid Karzai
Demands foreign troops
Withdrawal from villages.

2013 June The US alliance focus
On military training and operations
On same day Taliban and US officials
Resumed talks in Doha, Qatar.
President Karzai defers negotiations with US.

May 27, 2014, Obama proclaims
Timetable for troop withdrawal
First phase 9,800 US forces
"The remnants of al Qaeda"
Freeing up resources
for counteracting terrorism.
The candidates trying to succeed
President Karzai
Promise to sign an agreement
Of security.

Ashraf Ghani newly elected President
Signs power pact
With his chief opponent,

Abdullah Abdullah who organized
Thousands of protesters
As he challenges voting results.
John Kerry establishes Abdullah
As executive over securities.
Taliban gains in countryside.
Obama sees as a welcome change.
Karzai complained against civilian casualties.
In US War efforts.

April 13, 2017, Donald Trump pass on
Decision authority to commanders.
Non-nuclear bomb in Islamic State militants
Complex in eastern Nangarhar
Providence.
Kabul goes throughs suicide attacks
As never before.

August 21, 2017, Trump address troops in Arlington, Va.
States decision to withdrawal
Will based on combat on ground.
Rather than 'timetable'
Combat restrictions relaxed.
UN reports civilian casualty's upturn.
Political settlement far off with Taliban.

Jan 2018 Taliban creates
terror attacks in Kabul.
115 people killed
Trump deploys troops to rural areas
Launches air strikes against
Opium labs, to cut off finances.
Pakistan assistance in harboring militicians
Ghani and Provincial Governor
Clash.

February 2018 US Taliban Peace Talks Progress
Trump plans to withdrawal
7,000 soldiers, half of total. Forces
In exchange for pledging
Not to harbor terrorist groups.

September 7, 2019, Trump breaks off talks
After US soldier killed in
Taliban attack.
Taliban says talks must begin again
Or more increase in deaths.

February 29, 2020, US Taliban sign Peace Agreement.
Cease fire not in agreement.
Taliban fighters attack Afghan security forces,
US responds with air strikes.
In southern province.
Helmand.

September 12, 2020, Taliban representatives
And Afghan government
To meet and civil society
In Doha. Qatar talks.
Afghan government release
5,000 Taliban prisoners.
Taliban says must be an Islamic system.

November 2020, US announces Withdrawal
From Afghanistan
Trump campaign promises.
The end of forever War,
NATO Secretary General
Jens Stoltenberg
Says to early
Could lead to terrorism.
The setup of Islamic State.

April 14, 2021, Biden wants to complete by 9/11.
"It's time to end America's longest War"
Not dependent on progress of Peace talks.
Washington will support
Security forces,
And Peace talk progress.

August 15, 2021, Afghanistan government
Dissolves.
As Taliban take Kabul.

October 7, 2021, Democrats and Republicans
In US Senate
Have reached an agreement
To extend the debt ceiling
Through September.
Avoiding an economic disaster
USA not being able to pay its bills.

Everyday women send me revealing photos
Asking for gift cards.
With proposition for sex and money.
This is Capitalism, they speak of Taliban.
That is why the Taliban exist.
Women in Capitalism
Only want wealth.

The capitalist politicians promote this
And encourage immigrants.
The old immigrants were not subsidized
By government
Bribed to come in America.

The CIA now as result of end of War
Turning its interest to China
It is a Capitalist organization
Which has no interest in American people.

Ghani left Kabul with $150 million in cash
Belonging to Afghan people
It was reported and now
Being probed.
Former Hamid Karzai
Has also admitted that
It was "not unusual" for CIA
To leave bags of cash for years,

The first meeting since the fall of Kabul.
The CIA deputy director, David Cohen.
Sat down Saturday, October 9, 2021,
And Sunday in Doha, the capital
Of Qatar with Taliban
To focus on terrorism.

Friday ISIS-K attacked Kunduz
Killed dozens.
The evacuation of foreign citizens, and Afghans.
"Issues of US national interest"

Taliban spokesperson Suhail Shaheen:
"Yes, there is a meeting to discuss
Bilateral agreement of Doha 2020."

A great neglected work of Robert Schumann
His 1843 secular oratorio 'Parodies Und die Peri'
Soloist, Chorus and Orchestra.

President Biden is the first to formally recognized
Indigenous People's Day.
"For generations, Federal policies
Systematically sought to assimilate
and displace Native people and eradicate
their Native cultures."
"Today we recognize Indigenous people'
Resilience and strength as well as
Immeasurable positive impact
That they have made on every aspect
Of American society."

Soon Rickers Island jail complex will be closed.
This year alone twelve inmates
Died. Lawlessness and
Decrepit physical grounds will end.

Small retailers having shortages
From supply system.
President Biden meeting
With industry leaders and port directors.
Shipping containers and unloaded ships
Piling up at ports,
Shortage of truck drivers to deliver products.

Marx talks about the fall of Capitalist system.
The Chinese Communist
Are now surpassing the Capitalist countries
Economically.

The raise In Minimum Wage is necessary
For citizens to be uplifted.
Yet inflation takes place as a result, prices rise.
A major flaw in Capitalistic system.

Siege of Capital, average citizens
United in acts of brutality.
Fighting with police guarding preventing entry.
They now are co-defendants
In a multitude of felonies.

The United Nations, the United States
And several European Nations
On Wednesday condemned
North Korea's recent missile test
And said Pyongyang's technical
Advances demonstrate
The imperative need to increase
Its nuclear sanctions, and economic.

North Korea is an independent Nation
And has right to free choice
Of the society it wishes to conduct
To defend itself against imperialist policies
Of United Nations and United States.

Zabiullah Mujahid, the Taliban's chief spokesperson,
Poverty in his country,
The US is to blame
For freezing government assets
His group wants to access.
The redemption of Humanitarian aid
Is being prevented.
"The U.S. should release our money
So, we can save more children."

The U.S. chief ambassador resigned.

Obama and Bruce Springsteen podcast.
Like Phil Murphy
the Governor of New Jersey.
Baraka Obama only
Appreciates Capitalist Pop Art.

Pakistani Prime Minister Imran Khan
Declared that the Taliban
Were "breaking the chain of slavery."
Pakistan continues to be
A major source of financial and
Logistical support
For Taliban
Despite pressure from USA.

The Rahbari Shura (The Taliban leadership)
Better known as
The Quetta Shura. Make decisions
For all "political and military affairs
Of the Emirate."
Currently led by Mawlawi Haibatullah Akhundzada
Malawi Hiatellid Akhundzada
Was presently leader.

Kabul. October 23, 2021.
The Taliban militants are at almost
Every street corners.
They are now the guardians'
Of the city.
ISIS is now the enemy.
ISIS-K is now trying
To undermine and infiltrate
The Taliban.

"Yes, 100%, he said, "We can completely
Guarantee security. For the Afghan people.

Fifty killed in suicide bombing
At a mosque in southern city
Of Kandahar, used by Shiite Muslims'

"We are all concerned" he said,
"It is extremely hard in our community,
No one wants to be attacked
While they pray."
"Yet he does not see ISIS-K as a real threat."

The first interview with
Former Afghanistan Ambassador
A chief negotiator with Taliban
Zalmay Khalilzad
Disagreed the agreement
He negotiated to withdraw
U.S. troops.
Disagreeing with direction of Biden Administration.
"One reason I felt the government
Is the debate, wasn't really?
As should be based on relations
And facts of what happened
And what was going to on
And what our alternatives were."

Certain alleged Capital rioters
Are acting as their attorneys
Of the 650 cases
More than five defendants
Have decided to represent themselves.
Eighty-three percent of all federal trials in 2019
Were found guilty.

NPR reporting publishing this
Did not point out the large amount
Of overcharged expensive.
Of law or their lawyers
Unwillingness to conduct
Their clients wish.

"It's time for the American people to hear
directly from the top fossil fuel executives
about how they manufactured and concealed
a global emergency while reaping trillions in
corporate profits" Rep. Carolyn Maloney

"What they're doing in expanding oil development
Is inconsistent with what they are claiming
they're going to do." Rep. Ro Khanna.

Majid Khan, 41, years old
Who was held in a CIA facility,
Known as 'black sites'
Made statements to a military jury:
"I thought I was going to die"
Forced to be for extended periods
Naked while being sexually assaulted,
Starvation, getting doused in icy water
Nearly drowning. In secret prisons overseas
Before being transferred
To Guantanamo in 2006.
He was forced fed through his rectum.
Citizen of Pakistan, attended
School in Baltimore.
Assisted in plans of terror, some never
Took place.
"The more I cooperated and told them,
The more I was tortured."
The agency was defended by President
George W. Bush.
President Obama terminated it in 2009.
"I have also tried to make up for the bad
I have done.
That is why I have plead guilty.
Cooperating with USA government."

A few days do not go by when a young woman
Contacts me online, who eventually
Want a 'gift cards.
The situation with Taliban
Is the opposite of Capitalist Christian.
I have since learned to deal with it
Not wasting time texting them back.
The two myths Eve and Pandora
Have much truth in them.
Yet this is a narrow view of women
Forged from the ancient societies
They lived in.
In New Jersey woman receive
Encouragement to fulfill their nature
Instincts, getting child support
Giving birth with someone
They have no interest in.
Now the Capitalist Attorneys represent Men
Against women who cannot afford
Attorneys. The men now collect.
The Attorneys see an opportunity to
To make a profit.

Haibatullah Akhundzada, the Supreme leader of
Taliban, spoke to supporters
In the southern city of Kandahar.
His first public appearance since his leadership
In 2016. He is the chief spiritual leader.
He has remained secluded.
On Saturday he visited the Darul Uloom madrassa.
To "speak to the brave solders and disciples,"
"May God reward the oppressed people of Afghanistan
Who fought the infidels, and the oppressors
For 20 years."
"My intention is to pray for you and pray for me."
He talks about success in the 'big test' of rebuilding
What is called the Islamic Emirate of Afghanistan.
"Let's pray that we come out of this big test successfully
May Allah help us stay strong."
Akhundzada was a low-profile religious figure when
A drone strike killed Mullah Akhtar Mansour.
He received backing from Al-Qaeda chief.
His public messages were limited to Islamic holidays.

His message was on September 7,
When he told the new government to
Uphold sharia law as they govern."
They responded that they would follow his advice
Therefore, will have a progressive government.

We were told by some on Halloween weekend
That a terrorist attack
Was being planned, hence we were alerted.
The real reasons behind
This alert was that those that
Sell arms and want to conduct
Imperialist policies
Have interest in alerts.
Attacks are possible though
If we continue to make enemies
With our policies.

Statements by President Joe Biden
On the House passage
Of the Bipartisan Infrastructure Investment
And Jobs Act.

"Tonight, we took a monumental step
forward as a nation."
"The United States House of Representatives
Passed the Infrastructure Investment Bill
That will create millions of jobs,
Turn climate crisis into opportunity,
And put us win the economic competition
For the twenty-first century.
It will create good-paying jobs that can't
Source out.
Jobs that will transform our transportation
System with the most significant
Investments in passenger and freight rail,
Roads, bridges, ports, airports,
And public transits in generations."
",,,replacing lead water pipes,,,
Make high-speed internet affordable
And available everywhere,,,
National network of electric vehicle
Charging stations across the country.
The passage of Build Back Better Act.
"It will lower bills for Healthcare, childcare,
Elder care, prescription drugs, and
Preschool. And middle-class families
Get a tax cut."
This bill is also fiscally responsible, fully paid for..."
Doesn't raise taxes a single cent
On anyone making less than $400,000 per year."

It is believed that the end of fighting,
In Afghanistan.
Will now take place in areas
Outside of major cities.
Little of the aid of billions of dollars
Ever reached these sites
The end of corruption and fighting.
Is seen with hope.
"Now there is no sound of shooting,
The war has ended, and we are happy
with the Taliban."
Said 72-year-old women
In remote farming district
In northern Balkh province.
A man tending his sons grave spoke,
"The men and women of this village
Are Taliban supporters,
Young and old."
"Now I'm satisfied,
Now there is no more infidels"
Da Afghanistan Breshna Sherkat (DABS)
Revealed a deal that would
Purchase 100-megawatt supply
In wake of electric crisis.
Iran is suppling electric power
After owing ninety million to
Uzbekistan, Tajikistan, and Turkmenistan.
The US government has frozen ten billion
Of Afghanistan are
Held of its central bank.

Inflation soared at an annual rate
Of 6.2% last month. More than triple
The Federal Reserve 2% preference.
Despite saying the fastest decrease in unemployment,
Wages up, savings up.
Which are due at least to the easing of Covid.
Prices are higher, especially gas.
Senator Joe Machin West Virginia Democrat
Tweeted "From the grocery store
To the gas pump. Americans know the inflation
Tax is real and DC can no longer ignore
The economic pain Americana feel every day."

In March 2019, the US military hid the killing
Of fifty or more women and children,
In Syria in its War on Islamic State.
A drone attack near Baghuz,
While searching for military targets,
For members.
Near a riverbank were women and children.
The drone dropped two bombs
After a US F15 E jetted across
In from of the drone,
Blocking its vision.
Most of the civilians were killed.

Two hundred some nations agreed at COP26 summit
In Glasgow. To lower
Carbon dioxide emissions in half
By end of decade.
To keep warming to 1.5 degree Celsius.
Wealthy nations are urged to "at least double"
Funding to the most susceptible Nations.

Portugal lawmakers added protection
To remote workers.
Employers can not
Communicate with them
during time off.

Tens of thousands of Afghan refugees
are living in indeterminate state
On US Military bases.
They do not have resources
For the upcoming winter
And do not know when
They will have permanent places
To live.
In Fort McCoy, Wisconsin, 13,000 refugees
Are staying needing clothes for the cold.
Since August 17, the departure has been hectic.
A vast amount has been children.
Volunteer and resettlement groups say
Bewildered and shorthanded.

Lack of administrations plans
How to get Afghan allies out
Of Afghanistan
The Homeland security has denied,
Stating everyone has been
given jackets.

There is a lack of vaccinations.
These complains to military staff
Are often met with hostility.

In Philadelphia, PA. more than four hundred homicides
Have been committed this year.
Is this happing in Kabul, Afghanistan?
The United States is freezing
Their funds in the central bank.
With these funds they could
Hold off the starvation that the UN says
Will ensue. The citizens who
Elected these representatives
Are responsible for this
Humanitarian disaster.

November 16, 2021, Taliban's officials
Said they stressed eleven suspects
Associated with ISIS-K,
Their weapons seized, thought to be
Involved in attack in Kabul
After Taliban takeover.
Ten more arrested a few days ago
In Kandahar province. Four hideouts
Were eliminated.

Afghan Shiites seek protection
From Taliban.
In front of a Shiite shrine in Kabul,
Four armed Taliban guards
As worshipers entered for Friday.
Prayers.
The Taliban are more moderate,
They no longer repress the Hazaras
As well as other ethnic sects.

Russian humanitarian aid arrives in Kabul.
Vietnam in UN debate
On crisis in Afghanistan
Request all nations to comply with
International humanitarian law,
With regards to Afghans.

Taliban destroys Daesh Islamic haven.
Killing two, and arresting others.

The US military leaders again try to
Obtain War funds from Congress
By creating fictional aggressions
By the Chinese government.
Resulting of Asian children attacked
On a subway in Philadelphia, PA.

The United States must begin to apprehend
That all nations have freedom
Of choice, they do not have
To accept Christian Capitalist democracy
In control of USA today.

An Iranian plane in Jalalabad Airport that reopened,
Aid of ten tons of humanitarian
Including, food, clothing, and medical supplies.
Iran has also sent to qandaur, balkh,
Kabul and herat.

Jalalabad, Afghanistan, the Taliban sent more
Thousand fighters utilized to Nangahar
In eastern provenance to **intensified** brutal
Violence in night raids against
Islamic state. Killing those that do not surrender

Pakistan's Prime Minister Imran Khan permitted passage
Of 50.000 tonnes (MT) of wheat from India.
The humanitarian aid assistance also
Allowing those Afghani's in India
To return after medical treatment.

European Union, on Monday, the 29th of November,
Will resume discussions in Doha
To secure humanitarian funds and
Potential diplomatic representation.
Nabila Massrali commission spokesperson confirmed.
The EU delegation stressed
That the Taliban must take meaningful steps
Toward an inclusive government,
Representative of rich and diverse
Afghan society.

In discussions in Doha, Qatar,
The Taliban delegation
Has raised desire that US administration
To unfreeze financial assets,
Allowing government to function
As economic crisis ensues.
The Taliban Abdul Qahar Balkhi, spokesperson
For Ministry of foreign Affairs..
That FM Muttaqi negotiated views
Political, economic, health, education,
Security, and humanitarian issues.
As well banking and liquidity,
Ending blacklist, and sanctions.

The United Nations has not approved
A seat at the world organization.
Sohail Shaheen, UN nominee,
Expressed In statements
"Why they should be targets of sanctions, pressures
And deprived of a seat in UN because they wanted
An Afghanistan, free of occupation and able to have
Positive relations with any country of the world based
On mutual interests."

The United Nations and its affiliates
Are conducting requirement evaluations
While distributing aid across Afghanistan.
In past seven days, they dispersed food
For 280.000 people in four provinces.
Winter assistance to 20,000
In Ghor, Kabul, and Parwan provinces

"The Islamic Emirate doesn't have good relations with the UN
And therefore, the UN is concerned about the aid and stresses
It should be directly handed over to the vulnerable people."

"The Islamic Emirate formed a committee to manage
The humanitarian aid. The committee active under
The Economic Ministry and will cooperate in the distribution
Of aid to vulnerable people."

Like Christianity, Jewish, Muslim, Buddhist, and Hindu religions
Are not necessary to live
a good happy life on this planet.
As for an 'after world,' if it does exist
It is not dependent on
Non or Vengeful 'God.'
A philosopher like Confucius is the way.

Today, December 4th, the Taliban foreign minister
Is meeting with the Chinese ambassador
To Kabul to talk about political affairs,
Humanitarian aid, trade and
Providing technical educational
To Afghan students,
This was the second such meetings.

December 5. The Taliban guaranteed to probe reports
Of executions and disappearance
Of police and intelligence officers
After taking over and declaring amnesty.
Any IEA members found violating
Amnesty degree will be penalized and prosecuted.
Instances will be investigated but rumors rejected.

It is December 8th. My poem must come to a completion.
Yesterday Presidents Biden and Putin
Met virtually. They discussed
The situation in Ukraine.
I do not believe in the invasion of Russia
Into this free Nation. Yet I understand
President Putin and the Russians fear of
USA's imperialist invasions since WW II.
Our Nation must live in an international
Community 'A falu'. The village of this planet.
Not the tyrannical world of Capitalist Christianity,
Which many of us live in here.

Secretary of State Blinken is a most intolerant
Blind eyed political leader.
He refuses to accept that the USA
Is the most decadent, and human rights Nation
Violator on this Planet.
I feel that this a fitting way to conclude this poem.
Everyday in cities and suburbs are homicides
Poverty and homelessness.
Decadent popular entertainment, which
Fuels all these violations against mankind.

Wang Yu Chinese ambassador to Afghanistan,
In transfer ceremony revealed
Three million doses of vaccines,
Medical supplies arrived in Kabul.
Emergency assistance, including flood
Winter supplies and medicine.
China is importing pine nuts
That farmers income will benefit equal
By hundred of million US dollars.
Liberty village in the largest the largest settlement
Of Department of Homeland Securities,
In McGuire-Dix-Lakehurst Bases.
Many refugees have been since August 15th.
It is a slow process that they have had to endure.

Secretary Blinken tweets about political prisoners
In other countries! As if there were none here.
I spent more than three months in a cell, twenty-three
And a half hour a day, plus
Five weeks awaiting transfer, not able
Produce bail because my carryon
Luggage was confiscated at US Customs.
Merely for speaking and writing.

Placards read "Let us eat" "Give us our money"
As protester chant "Unfreeze our funds"
In the streets of Kabul Tuesday.
The USA continues to hold on to assets,
And sanction against
International Principles.
Democratic US House members sent a letter
To President Biden and Treasury Department,
That they stand with allies and
Humanitarian authorities, to unfreeze funds.

Former Lt. Col. Stuart Scheller who went on Facebook
Video criticizing US military leadership,
After losing his personal colleague
In terrorist attack, in the withdrawal.
"growing discontent and contempt" and
"ineptitude of the foreign policy level."
Was discharged Thursday, December 23rd, 2021.
Comminating for being locked up for five days,
"without basic items in prison."
Revealed he would conduct a 'media blitz'
Beginning on January 4th
With Tucker Carlson of Fox News.

Kazakhstan, Afghanistan discusses possibilities
Improving trade and economic cooperation.
Kazakhstan has been a supplier of grain and flour
To Afghanistan. While it imports Afghan
Fruits and vegetables.

The cultivation of oranges is at an orchard
In the Bati Kot district of Nangarhar
Province of eastern region.
The growing of citrus, lemons, and oranges
Would bring excellent incomes to farmers.
The increase in harvest was
More than 2020.

After months in locations overseas
Approximately 3,000 people wait
To be processed without possessions or paperwork.
83.000 Afghans and American citizens arrived in US,
Estimating cost at 4.2 billion through December
Many do not still have cloths or medicine.
Congress has supplied an additional 4.3 billion.
48.000 Afghans have been resettled
Yet tens of thousands have not relocated from bases.
'unemployment and spending hours walking
Children to schools with no autos.
Many of do not have food stamps and are starving,
In hotels, Airbnb, temporary housing and churches.'

Quotes of verses from Quran and hidiths
Are ridiculous. Which the Ministry
Of Virtue and Prevention of Vice
Concerning beards.
Muhammad was a vain prophet who has brought
Much hate and War besides love
To the world.

The first shipment of 1,500 metric tons of wheat
Passed through the border from Pakistan.
The total package includes 50.000 metric tons
Of wheat, winter shelter and medical aid.

Chinese Foreign Minister Wang Yi
Stated that irresponsible withdrawal
By USA from Afghanistan has brought
Serious humanitarian catastrophe
To Afghan people and instability to area.
The failure of the 'democratic transformation'
Of Afghans after years of War.
Should not have to suffer further.
China has "reached out to Afghan people
With emergency humanitarian assistance"

India has supplied its next set of
Humanitarian assistance.
500.000 doses of COVID-19 vaccine.
Another batch next week.
Wheat and medical assistance
In coming weeks.

The United States of America
Its leaders and people have not
Made after twenty years any assistance.
Wanting only to impose
Christian Capitalist democracy on its society.
Creating suffering and grief!

THE END